PRIDE OVER PASSION

DREW A. INGLE

5 RULES TO CAREER SATISFACTION

Pride Over Passion

This book is a work of nonfiction; however, some stories and analogies are made-up through imagination to show examples of ideas. Any resulting resemblance to persons living or dead in these examples is entirely coincidental and unintentional. Additionally, the advice and strategies found within this book may not be suitable for every situation or career. This work is sold with the understanding that the author, publisher, and distributor are not held responsible for the advice in this book being a guarantee to improve career satisfaction.

Copyright © 2021 by Drew Ingle. All rights reserved.

No part of this publication may be reproduced, distributed, or transmitted in any form or by any means, including photocopying, recording, or other electronic or mechanical methods, without the prior written permission of the publisher/author, except in the case of brief quotations embodied in reviews and certain other non-commercial uses permitted by copyright law.

Book ideation and writing by Drew Ingle
Final editing by Elise Gallagher
Cover design by Chris Schatzman

ISBN: 978-1-7365693-0-6 (Paperback)
ISBN: 978-1-7365693-1-3 (Hardback)
ISBN: 978-1-7365693-2-0 (eBook)

Any questions, comments, or feedback regarding *Pride Over Passion* can be addressed to: PrideOverPassion@gmail.com

*This book is dedicated to my daughter, Carly,
may you find a rewarding and satisfying career.*

Pride Over Passion

Contents

Introduction..9

Rule One: Don't Rely On Passion Alone......................17

Rule Two: 95% Practice 5% Game............................29

Rule Three: Set Goals...37

Rule Four: Expectation Hierarchy............................51

Rule Five: Pride In Progress..................................63

Closing Remarks..77

Acknowledgments..81

Notes...85

Pride Over Passion

Introduction

There is an ever-increasing problem ripping through the modern workforce: career dissatisfaction. What makes this problem modernly unique is that it is no longer limited to those who have failed to pursue their passion, in fact, quite the opposite. That is because society has progressively cornered passion into an end-all be-all solution to happiness. Phrases such as, "follow your passion and you will never work a day in your life" have created the notion that our passions alone hold the key to a consistently satisfying career. While there is no arguing that our passion plays an important role in enjoying our work, it is our overreliance of its abilities that has become our Achilles' heel to dissatisfaction. I would unfortunately have to experience this dilemma firsthand before finding a distinctive way to overcome it.

Upon graduating college, I was ecstatic to start my career in a job that I was truly passionate about. I went into that job expecting my passion to create consistent motivation and satisfaction within my work as I had no reason to believe otherwise. Over time, however, I began to experience inconsistencies to my satisfaction. Instead of "never working a day in my life," I found that many projects, tasks, and assignments felt more like work rather than pleasure. This uncertainty of satisfaction eventually led me to question whether or not I had properly pursued my passion. While the good days still outweighed the bad, the constant feeling of unmet expectations slowly caused me to become unengaged and disillusioned in a job I had previously loved.

This mindset grew progressively worse, until one day I made the decision to look for a new career opportunity. In my mind, a new job was the only way I could still find that "never work a day in your life" experience. I knew before I could make such a significant life changing decision, however, that I would need to seek some professional advice. To do so, I reached out to a few of my mentors in the hopes of receiving some strong direction and input towards my pursuit of passion. Little did I know that the advice I would receive from one of my most trusted mentors would be the spark to ignite a completely new way of thinking towards my career.

After sitting down and explaining my circumstances to this mentor, I was eager to hear the words of wisdom he had to offer in return. To my surprise, he did not respond with any direct statements or thoughts. Instead, he responded with a series of thought-provoking questions that initially felt very out of place.

The first question he asked me was, "Did you enjoy every day of playing football?" While this mentor knew about my previous passion of playing football, I was confused what that experience had to do with my current circumstances.

Humoring his question, I responded by saying, "Yes, I loved it, but what does that have to do with seeking a new job?"

Instead of answering my question, my mentor asked his question once again, this time in more depth, "Did you enjoy every day of playing football, the practices, the drills, the conditioning?" Before I could even answer, he asked a follow-up question, "Were you just as excited to play in the games as you were your practices?"

I started to understand where he was going with his questions. I replied by saying, "My most exciting moments were, of course, playing in the games, as practices were rarely exciting."

With that, he asked me his last and most important question, "If your excitement was not consistent across your passion for football and you never considered quitting, why, then, are you considering quitting your current passion due to inconsistent excitement?"

It was a valid question that I had never considered before, and it certainly made me reflect on my previous experience of passion compared to my current one. It helped me realize the similarities between these two experiences. During football, I was always excited to play in the games. Playing in the games was the core of my passion and why I initially participated in the sport. Similarly, in my job, I was excited to do what I was most passionate about. There was a flip-side to all this excitement though: the unfavorable tasks required of me in each experience.

Football practices were a tiring drudgery that, at best, were a watered-down version of what I loved most… playing in the games. I realized that just like those football practices, there were circumstances within my job that were less interesting or exciting. There was one glaring difference between these two experiences, though; I had somehow found satisfaction in even the most undesirable football practices. This comparison was where the similarities ended, as I was certainly not finding satisfaction in the unmotivating and unfavorable aspects of my job. I knew that replicating my prior ability to create satisfaction in my football practices was my best shot at regaining consistent satisfaction in my career. I just needed to learn how I had achieved such a feat.

After some very deep thought and reflection, I realized that I had unknowingly applied a handful of unique mindsets towards my previous football experience. What made these mindsets unique was their ability to stay untouched by the traditional concepts of passion. Unlike the "never work a day in your life" expectation I had been applying towards my career, I understood that sports required an investment to do what I loved most. I accepted that playing football would not mean consistently playing in games but would require my dedication of hard work throughout my practices to reach those moments of peak satisfaction. In this way, I never thought twice about practices being less exciting. It was this mindset combined with a unique set of goals and expectations that allowed me to become less reliant on my games as my only source of satisfaction and recognize additional opportunities to create enjoyment in my work.

These mindsets created a foundation of achievements that allowed me to take pride in the progress of my work. It did not matter whether it was rain or shine, that sense of pride I had in my football practices always helped me maintain a feeling of satisfaction over any unfavorable circumstance. I knew that this collection of mindsets was the answer I had been looking for to overcome my current reliance of passion for satisfaction. Now, all I could do was hope that these mindsets translated over from my football experience into my business career with the same results.

With this in mind, I decided not to chase my satisfaction through a new job but instead work on reestablishing my satisfaction within my current career. I realized I had properly pursued my passion—I had just failed to properly pursue my satisfaction. Over the next few years, I would tirelessly and painstakingly work on applying these mindsets into the "practices" of my career. I knew that creating a consistently satisfying career would not happen overnight, but eventually, I found myself becoming more consistently satisfied in my work. I molded my previous mindsets that I had applied towards my football practices into five specific rules. These unique rules offered me a way to overcome even the most unfavorable and unsatisfying circumstances of my career. While my passion was still a key element to enjoying my work, I now had the ability to create satisfaction outside of my direct interests.

Why It Matters

In the midst of my experience with dissatisfaction and the creation of my five rules, I found that many of my friends, past classmates, and colleagues were all struggling with similar circumstances within their own careers. I had friends constantly changing jobs, some more than once in the same year, all seeking that consistent satisfaction within their work. I knew past classmates that landed their dream jobs only to feel disillusioned after their expectations of consistent satisfaction went unmet. In fact, the number of people I knew dealing with some level of dissatisfaction within their career grew so high that I became curious to learn how widespread this issue truly reached. After some basic research on the topic, I would become absolutely dumbfounded by just how significant this problem was in our society.

According to a Gallop World Poll, 85% of the world's workforce is unengaged in their work.[1] Additionally, The Conference Board found that in the past decade over half of American workers on average have been unsatisfied in their jobs.[2] If these statistics were not concerning enough, a study done by Mental Health America and the Faas Foundation found that 70% of employed workers are thinking about, or actively looking for new jobs due to low engagement in their work.[3] Reading these statistics put me in a state of disbelief. Here I was thinking I had done something wrong in my pursuit of passion when the overwhelming majority of the workforce was struggling with similar experiences. How is it, then, that we keep preaching the "never work a day in your life" motto when there is a clear disconnect between following our passions and obtaining a consistently satisfying career?

After years of working on and perfecting my five rules to career satisfaction, I knew I could not sit idly by while millions around me were still struggling with dissatisfaction in their careers. If I could help even a fraction of those feeling unsatisfied, then I could still make a significant impact on this modern-day problem. With that, I set out to write my five rules meticulously and methodically into this book. Each rule has been carefully crafted to highlight the most important information and ideas needed to create a mental mind shift towards one's career. It is also important to note that these rules are not just five lessons expressed through my own personal experiences, but are full of reputable studies and in-depth research on the subject to help highlight the scientific and psychological importance these rules carry in our way of thinking. No longer should we be susceptible to our circumstances and misguided expectations of passion. It is time we take back control of our careers; it is time we take back control of our satisfaction.

The 5 Rules To Career Satisfaction

Rule One: Don't Rely On Passion Alone

Rule Two: 95% Practice 5% Game

Rule Three: Set Goals

Rule Four: Expectation Hierarchy

Rule Five: Pride In Progress

Rule One:
Don't Rely On Passion Alone

"You will never change your life until you step out of your comfort zone; change begins at the end of your comfort zone."

- Roy T. Bennett

There is no arguing that our passions are a great tool to utilize within our careers. However, whether we realize it or not, relying on passion alone can put us in a comfort zone of limited satisfaction. We can become so fixed on the promise of our passion that we avoid any type of work that does not fit our immediate interest. The irony is that this avoidance of temporary dissatisfaction can lead to greater dissatisfaction in the long-term of our career. That is why it is crucial that we educate ourselves on the mental boundaries that are created from an overreliance on passion, the consequences of these boundaries, and how they can deter us from maximizing our career satisfaction.

Passion Comfort Zones

What does it mean to over rely on passion in our careers and what are the consequences for having such a narrow-minded approach towards our work? Psychologists at Stanford University and Yale-NUS College wanted to understand this very dilemma when they conducted a series of studies to observe how a "fixed" (tunnel vision approach to passion) and a "growth" (open-minded approach to passion) impacted one's thought processes, expectations, and actions towards work.[4] What the psychologists found was shocking and concerning for those over relying on passion. Their studies found that a "fixed" mindset towards passion creates three specific boundaries of satisfaction that can lead to a significant consequence within our career. By studying these boundaries, we can begin the process of breaking free from our passion comfort zones.

Boundary One: Limited Interests

The first mental boundary created from a fixed mindset is believing that our passions are the only way to find interest and, therefore, satisfaction within our work. As stated in the Stanford study, "a fixed theory reduces interest outside people's preexisting interests." [5] In other words, when we focus on our passion as the only source of satisfaction within our career, we unsurprisingly limit ourselves to alternative interests or opportunities. While focusing on what we care about most might not sound problematic, it is this exclusivity that can hinder our ability to maximize our satisfaction. How can we ever expect to gain a career's worth of satisfaction if we are never willing to expand our horizons of interest?

Imagine if we approached relationships with our friends the same way we approached our passion. If we only expected our friends to do what we wanted and never considered investing in their interests over our own, we would risk two potential outcomes. First, we would risk our attitude being so poor from the disappointment of not doing what we wanted that our friends would not enjoy spending time with us, as well as creating our own dissatisfaction. Second, we would risk our friends doing only what we wanted simply to keep us happy until they would inevitably feel neglected. Both scenarios would eventually leave us with broken relationships where we might get what we want in the moment but, at the end of the day, our long-term relationship, and the satisfaction that comes with it, is lost.

Our careers are no different. We cannot expect to maximize our career satisfaction by having a narrow-minded approach towards the work we consider to be satisfying. If we only allow ourselves to enjoy a certain form of work, then we are shutting the door to any further opportunities of satisfaction. Even the best dream jobs will require work outside of our direct interests, so how do we expect to maximize our satisfaction by avoiding such situations? If we want to build a long-term satisfying career, then we must see the benefit of investing in alternative interests. Like maintaining a friendship, this means that we must occasionally sacrifice our initial wants to ensure a long-term relationship with our career.

Boundary Two: Limitless Motivation

When it comes to following our passion, motivation often seems easy to find. However, just because motivation typically goes hand-in-hand with the work we enjoy, it does not mean that motivation is consistently guaranteed when following our passion. This is the false reality that those with a "fixed" mindset tend to expect from a career they are passionate about. The Stanford study found that a fixed mindset "leads people to anticipate that a passion will provide limitless motivation." [6] This means when we over rely on passion, we are putting the power of our motivation in the hands of our circumstances. What happens then, when we face an unfavorable circumstance within our passion and we need motivation the most?

The answer lies in the relationship that we share with our significant other. Imagine what would happen if we similarly expected our spouse to make us happy no matter the circumstances. Such as following our passion, there are going to be days when this expectation simply cannot be fulfilled. For example, when our spouse is having a bad day, do we expect him/her to still make us happy, or do we see the need to set aside our wants and invest in his/her happiness? We, of course, see the need to invest back into his/her happiness. Imagine, however, if we viewed our relationships like a fixed mindset towards passion. We would not only become dissatisfied by our spouse not working to make us happy but would simultaneously weaken the longevity of that relationship by never investing back into his/her happiness.

This is exactly what we risk when expecting limitless motivation from our passion. When faced with a lack of motivation, we cannot afford to become upset and walk away from a situation believing it is our passion's responsibility to motivate us. If we want to have long-term satisfaction, then we must see the variability of motivation that comes with following our passion. Yes, our passions can strongly motivate us to do work we enjoy, but when our passions are not aligned with our unfavorable circumstances it becomes our responsibility, just like the relationship with our spouse, to invest back into our work so that we can maintain a long-term relationship with our career.

Boundary Three: Limited Difficulties

The type of work we define as "difficult" is different for everyone, but for those with a "fixed" mindset, "difficult" tends to be something that they believe should be nearly nonexistent in a career they are passionate about. As the psychologist within the Stanford study would find, those with a fixed mindset often believed that following their passion would limit the feeling of difficulty they would experience within their work.[7] This does not necessarily mean that they expected to face zero difficulties, but that those difficulties would feel easier and less challenging than those outside of their passion.[8] In other words, when people have an over reliance on passion, they expect their passion to create an easier path of work simply because they are doing something they enjoy. The problem here is that our interests do not limit difficulties, they just make those difficulties worth enduring.

This way of thinking is similar to expecting the disagreements with those close to us to be easy because we share a relationship with them. Just because someone is close to us does not mean we will share any easier disagreements than with those of a stranger. The difference between a disagreement with a stranger and someone close to us is our willingness to work through those disagreements and actively resolve them. Similarly, when it comes to our careers, we must understand that certain difficulties will not become any easier just because they fall under our passion, in fact, following our passion could potentially mean pursuing even more difficult work. The difference between our passion and another career is that our passions, like those relationships with our friends and family, are worth fighting for. Following our passions will not mean doing what is easy, but committing to something worth preserving even when faced with difficulties.

Consequence: Questioning Interests

Using the analogies of treating our passions like relationships, we can clearly see the consequences for over relying on passion. If we only believed that satisfying relationships could come from our friends doing exclusively what we wanted, that it is our significant other's responsibility to constantly make us happy, and our disagreements with those close to us should always be easy, then we would undoubtedly walk away from any meaningful relationship due to unmet expectations. When it comes to the relationships with our careers, the psychologists at Stanford University and Yale-NUS College concluded that the consequences of expecting our passions to be the only path for interesting work, limitless motivation, and lack of difficulty are very similar to this analogy.

They found that "a fixed theory leads to a sharper decline in interest—as if the person comes to think that the topic was not their interest after all." [9] In other words, just as someone might believe a friendship isn't right if their unrealistic expectations go unmet 24/7, we too can risk walking away from a passion by unrealistically expecting it to offer us consistent satisfaction.

Like our relationships, our careers require sacrifice and investments to grow. If we give into the idea that our passions are a walk in the park that offer us unlimited satisfaction, then we risk walking away from what we love most at the first sign of dissatisfaction and disappointment. If we do not fix this mentality, then we will never be able to maintain a meaningful relationship with our passion. Instead, we will always search for that unrealistic expectation of passion at the end of the rainbow sacrificing our full potential of satisfaction along the way.

Facing Our Boundaries

As we will learn throughout the remainder of these rules, consistent satisfaction does not come from our passion alone but rather from overcoming the unfavorable circumstances of our career. If we are to overcome these circumstances and create satisfaction, then we must be prepared to face the subconscious temptations that exist at the edge of our boundaries of passion. I say subconscious temptations because research has shown that neurological activity in the mesolimbic dopamine system of our brains can actively motivate us towards a feeling of reward, even if that reward is temporary.[10] It is this subconscious drive for a feeling of "reward" that can unknowingly hold us back from long-term satisfaction if we do not become aware of it.

Whether we know it or not, this region of our brain is constantly tempting us to maintain a "feel good" state of mind. The greater the "feel good reward," the greater motivation our brain will push us toward that activity. On the surface, this makes sense. Our body is telling us to avoid unfavorable situations that do not give us pleasure and pursue ones that do. At first, this might sound like an ideal instinct to have, however, in our modern world it can drastically limit our career satisfaction by boxing us into a comfort zone of passion.

For example, a study conducted by psychologists, Peter Milner and James Olds, observed this natural phenomenon. Milner and Olds placed electrodes in the brains of rats, specifically in the mesolimbic dopamine region. The rats were then placed in a box with two levers. One lever provided food and water while the other would trigger a shock to their brain releasing that natural sense of "feel good reward." Over the course of the study, some rats began to only press the lever stimulating this feeling of internal reward. These rats did so to the point of collapse, choosing the rewarding shock over essential food and water.[11]

While it might not be surprising that a rat chose to simulate its reward centers occasionally over food and water, it is surprising that they did it to the point of dehydration and starvation. This shows the dramatic override this region of our brain can have on our actions and reasonable thinking. Besides using logic to consider the long-term satisfaction that food could have on their overall sustainability of life, the rats gave into the temporary desire to satisfy this subconscious motivation time and time again. This showed that the rat's mesolimbic dopamine system constantly motivated them towards what felt good, rather than what was good for them.

As much as we would like to think we act differently than these rats, we are not as far off as we might think.

While we are obviously not skipping meals from this type of temptation, we are constantly choosing what feels good over what is good for us. A simple example is going to the gym. Everyday people actively give in to the temptation to sit on the couch and watch TV after a long day of work instead of going to the gym. Logic and reason would tell us that going to the gym is better for us and has the potential to increase our long-term satisfaction. However, our brains are more focused on our momentary satisfaction, always trying to avoid any feeling of discomfort causing us to be subconsciously motivated to stay home and watch TV. While we might experience a small sense of satisfaction from relaxing on the couch in the moment, that unmemorable evening will pale in comparison to the satisfaction we could have gained from committing to the gym over the long-term.

Unfortunately, we often give into similar temptations within our careers. Just like the rats, we choose what feels good in the moment rather than committing to what is good for us in the long-run. When we face our boundaries of limited interest, limited motivation, and increased difficulties, we reach the limit of this temptation. Our brains want us to turn back towards what is safe and comfortable because it is trying to maintain a constant state of "feel good reward." That is why we must acknowledge this internal battle if we want to overcome these boundaries of passion and make the necessary sacrifices to maximize our long-term satisfaction. When we understand that our brains are not focused on a five-year plan for satisfaction, but are instead focused on a five-minute plan to satisfaction, we can begin to fight back these temptations and break free from our passion comfort zone.

Finding Our Personal Comfort Zone

Now that we understand the typical boundaries created from over relying on passion, and the hurdles we will face when we try to break through them, it is crucial that we pinpoint our own personal boundaries that exist in our unique careers. To do this, we should look closely at the "Arousal Theory of Motivation" as a close comparison to our boundaries of passion. The arousal theory of motivation states that we each have "an optimal level of arousal that we all try to maintain. If we are under-aroused, we become bored and will seek out some sort of stimulation. On the other hand, if we are over-aroused, we will engage in behaviors to reduce our arousal." [12]

Similarly, we each have our own unique passion comfort zones where we experience limits of interests in our work. Just like the arousal theory, we can become bored or overwhelmed with a task at hand causing us to turn back towards our comfort zone. These are the moments when we face specific tasks, projects, or assignments that we believe are not motivating enough or are too difficult to be considered part of our passion. As such, we avoid these circumstances falling back to what "feels good" rather than investing in our long-term satisfaction. This is what rule one is all about, finding and recognizing these boundaries of passion so that we can begin the process of overcoming them. After these boundaries have been determined within our career, we can apply the remaining four rules as we begin to create a consistently satisfying career.

Rule Two:
95% Practice 5% Game

"The chief cause of failure and unhappiness is trading what you want most for what you want right now."

- Zig Ziglar

While rule one was about finding our limits of passion, rule two is about understanding the level of investment required of us outside of those limits and the reward for doing so. This investment is also not for the faint of heart. In a world filled with instant gratification, get rich quick schemes, and everything at our doorstep in a day, it can become easy to fall back into our passion comfort zones at the first sign of dissatisfaction besides powering through a challenge. If we genuinely want to maximize our satisfaction, then we must see the long-term reward for investing in our unfavorable circumstances.

An Athlete Analogy

A great analogy for looking at the investment required of us outside of our passion comfort zones is comparing our careers to that of an athlete. It does not matter if it is an Olympian athlete or Minor League athlete as they all share similar experiences of highs and lows that we do within a business career. The difference, however, is that athletes tend to have an alternative idea of following their passions than we do in the business world. Athletes have a clearer understanding of what is required of them if they want to participate in what they love most. Where many people expect their passion to be a consistent experience of doing what they love, athletes recognize that their sport will be a series of practices and games. The games are, of course, the highlight of their career, the moments that excite, motivate, and interest them the most. The practices, on the other hand, are far less exciting but still a necessary investment that must be made if they want to maximize their satisfaction.

What is interesting about an athlete's experience of practices and games is that they will spend a very small fraction of their overall career participating in their core interest. In fact, the amount of time an athlete spends at practice can easily add up to the 90th percentile of their overall career, while only about 5% of their time will be spent playing in an actual game. With such an uneven balance of time getting to do what they love most, how do athletes still enjoy their overall experience?

For starters, athletes recognize and accept this uneven balance going into their sport. Unlike a traditional job, there is not a "never work a day in your life" expectation. In a sport, athletes go into that career fully aware of the time commitment required of them outside of their games. Second, athletes recognize the benefit of trading what they want in the moment for what they want most. Even though practices are not the highlight of their satisfaction, maximizing their overall satisfaction would not be possible without investing in their practices. For example, an athlete could easily skip practice giving into his/her desire to do what feels good in the moment. When it would come time to play in the game, however, he/she would be significantly underprepared risking significant disappointment and dissatisfaction from the loss of a game. As a consequence, the athlete would have sacrificed what mattered most to him/her by giving into the temptation of temporary satisfaction.

Therefore, athletes recognize that it is nearly impossible to maximize their satisfaction without investing in their practices. While practices might not always be the most satisfying part of their career, it is only by investing in these moments that their overall satisfaction can be increased. This means athletes are less focused on the uneven balance of time doing what they love most and are more focused on the overall feeling of satisfaction that comes from investing in that time. That is why we too must stop focusing on how often we are "practicing" in our career, while focusing more on the return on investment that our "practices" offer us towards our overall satisfaction. When we do this our "practices" no longer become a burden to our satisfaction, but rather an opportunity to maximize it.

Translating To The Business World

A great real-world example of applying this "games" vs. "practice" mentality in our everyday work is by looking at an Apple Incorporated team's experience of building the first iPhone software. This team of Apple engineers was playing their passion or "sport" on arguably one of the best tech teams there is. They knew being on this team meant raising the bar in everything they did and doing so would often require working outside of their direct interests through "practices." In this example, the team was about to discover what it meant to truly endure "practice" to win a "game."

Greg Christie, former Apple Vice President of Human Interface, and Scott Forstall, former Apple Senior Vice President of iPhone Operating Systems, discussed some of these moments of "practices" and "games" when it came to working on the original iPhone prototype software in an interview with the *Wall Street Journal*. As Scott Forstall recalled, the team was gearing up for an early model of their software when Steve Jobs wanted to observe their progress. Forstall stated that Jobs' first impression was "this isn't good enough" and told the team they would have to do better if they wanted to be a part of the iPhone's development.[13]

As a result, Jobs gave the team two weeks to come up with something better, or he was going to give the project to another team.[14] At that moment, it was like the team had lost its first big game of satisfaction. The team was passionate about its work and knew that in order to win the "Super Bowl" of projects it needed to perform better. The members now had to go back to the drawing board and start giving it their all at "practice" if they wanted to win their next big "game".

Forstall explained that for the next two weeks the team worked over 168 hours with many members staying in a hotel near the office just so they could get some decent rest between their work.[15] It would have been easy for anyone on that team to fall back into their passion comfort zones, giving into the temptation to avoid any feeling of dissatisfaction. They could have decided that working 17-hour days did not "feel good" and was, therefore, not worth the discomfort. They knew, however, that the "game" they were working towards was bigger than any temporary dissatisfaction. They knew that winning this game was an opportunity to maximize their satisfaction, outweighing any discomfort they were experiencing in the moment. That is why for those next two weeks, the team pushed through their practice knowing what reward could be waiting for them on the other side if they properly invested their energy.

When the two weeks ended, the team came confidently prepared for the next "game" proud of their work. When they presented the new software concept they had worked tirelessly on to Jobs, he was blown away by the user interface they had created.[16] The feeling of satisfaction that this team must have felt from hearing one of the greatest business leaders being impressed by their work must have been extraordinary. Not only that, but they now had the pride of creating something that would be part of a timeless and historical product. Because they had not walked away from this challenge when it did not "feel good" in the moment, they were able to experience a new level of satisfaction that could only come from winning a "game." This level of satisfaction did not come from a lack of challenges but rather from conquering them. Even though these challenges might have been stressful and unsatisfying in the moment, overcoming them created a feeling of satisfaction unmatched by any comfort zone.

Investing In Our "Practices"

When we over rely on passion for satisfaction, we can risk limiting what we are willing to endure outside of our interests. By viewing our passion as a series of "games" and "practices" we allow ourselves to see the necessary investment required of us outside our direct interests to reach our peak satisfaction of passion. That is why we must stop expecting our passions to be a never-ending experience of "games" or we will inevitably become disappointed in our career. When we understand that following our passion means investing in our "practices" to better enjoy the "games" of our career, then we are headed on the right path for creating consistent satisfaction in our work.

Rule Three:
Set Goals

"If you want to live a happy life, tie it to a goal, not to people or things."

- Albert Einstein

Now that we understand the time commitment and investment required of us to reach the "games" of our career, we must learn how to create satisfaction along that journey. Doing so will require a handful of techniques, but some of the most important will be setting three specific and unique types of goals within our "practices." That is because all the rules, tips, and tricks in the world cannot help someone find consistent satisfaction in his/her work if he/she is not setting goals. Without goals, our "practices" would have no purpose, and without purpose, we would have no drive to overcome our unfavorable circumstances. As such, we would inevitably fall back to our passion comfort zones settling for temporary satisfaction.

Unfortunately, goal setting is far less common than one would think. According to a study done by Statistic Brain, 55% of Americans are either infrequently setting goals or never setting them period.[17] What is shocking about this study, outside of the obvious, is the similarity between this statistic and the number of people unsatisfied in their jobs. As stated within the introduction, the average rate of unsatisfied workers has been just over half of the American workforce in the past decade, meaning that the percentage of people not setting goals is remarkably similar to the percentage of people not satisfied in their jobs. Is it a coincidence, then, that these numbers are so close together, or might there be something to goal setting and job satisfaction?

Unsurprisingly, research has already proven that goal setting can improve our well-being, showing us the importance of setting goals to create satisfaction in our work.[18] Unfortunately, the advice typically given on goal setting focuses on a traditional "one size fits all" mentality. This traditional mindset of setting a goal and simply going after it does not always work in our favor when faced with the boundaries of passion. What we need is a new viewpoint, a re-imagining of our goals if we want to commit ourselves to overcome the unfavorable circumstances of our career. Enter the three supporting goal techniques. These goals do not undercut traditional goal setting but are instead an additional method to goal setting to assist us in our pursuit of a consistently satisfying career.

Pre-Qualifying Goals

A starting line is harder to cross than a finish line. This may sound like a ridiculous statement until we sit back and really think about what it takes for someone to put his/her foot on a starting line of a race. We often consider a race as going from point A to point B when in reality, the finish line of a race is really point Z with the starting line closer to point X than point A. Why? Because the race itself is only the tip of the iceberg compared to the overall work required to cross that finish line. The amount of time, energy, strength, and determination needed to even qualify for a race is often more demanding than the race itself. This is not to discredit how demanding the race will be, but at the end of the day, the race only requires a fraction of the effort than what it took to prepare for it.

Take, for example, the difference in time there is in preparing for a triathlon than actually competing in one. On average, it takes about three hours for trained competitors to complete the swimming, biking, and running portions of a triathlon. Accomplishing this does not happen by simply waking up one day, setting a goal to participate in a triathlon, and then competing in one that very same day. Such a task requires tremendous amounts of training and preparation both mentally and physically. The recommended amount of time to train for a triathlon is about 8-12 weeks for at least 4-6 hours a week, meaning a competitor is easily spending over 50 hours to participate in just three hours. In other words, for a competitor to accomplish his/her end goal of completing a race, he/she will have spent nearly all of his/her time outside of the race itself.

This analogy closely resembles our practice/game mentality because that is exactly how this goal should be used within our careers. We must acknowledge that when we set a goal to win a "game," enduring our "practices" can be more difficult than the game itself. If we do not establish this mindset, we can easily find ourselves showing up at the starting line of a race dangerously underprepared.

A great example of this way of thinking is looking back at the 45% of Americans who did actually set goals from that Statistic Brain study. Their study found that many of those who did set goals were not committed to finishing them. In fact, a quarter of the people who set goals gave up within the first week and over half gave up six months into their goals.[19]

I would argue that these people did not properly prepare for their race beforehand. They had good intentions by wanting to compete in their triathlon, metaphorically speaking, but were not properly prepared for what that race required of them. Instead, they viewed their goal like a race that they could just show up to the day of and complete. Without the right prequalifying mindset, they were too weak to overcome their temptations of their passion comfort zone giving up before they could ever finish their "race."

It is time we stop giving up on our goals from a lack of preparation. This does not mean that our finish lines should change, but how we approach them should. We cannot confidently show up to a "race" without first knowing we put in the work to endure what lies ahead of us. The next time we set a big goal within our career, we must understand that the work we do in preparation for that goal is just as important, if not more, than the work we put in during the goal itself.

Staircase Goals

One of the biggest challenges we will face when setting goals at "practice" is not giving into the temptation of believing we did "just enough." Let us say, for example, a group of people set a goal to climb the staircase of the Burj Khalifa, currently the world's tallest building located in Dubai, United Arab Emirates. How many people would push themselves to the top of those 2,900+ stairs and how many would be content with reaching a specific floor before stepping off the staircase? Not everyone's motivation to reach a goal is the same because not every goal is created equally. The motivation to reach the top floor may be greater for some than others even though they all had the same end goal in mind.

Setting goals in our career is no different. I would argue that many people set goals they genuinely intend to reach but find themselves stepping off the staircase because they feel they have accomplished "just enough" towards their goal due to their lack of interest. How, then, can we ever expect to maximize our satisfaction by stepping off our "staircase" early? We might tell ourselves we were content with the level we reached when really, we know it was our desire to fall back on what "feels good" that ceilinged our satisfaction.

That is why we must acknowledge that every career, job, goal, or task will have "easy out" moments where the door will be wide open when we feel like giving into the boundaries of our comfort zone. With each step up our staircase, we push the limits of our comfort zone further and further making the doors out more inviting the higher we go. We think if the first half of the journey was this hard, the second half will only be that much more difficult so why not enjoy the satisfaction of stepping off the staircase? Maybe if we step off the staircase at this task, assignment, or project then we will be satisfied enough in our efforts.

When we get into this "just enough" or "easy out" mentality, we have already lost the opportunity to maximize our satisfaction. We are letting the measurement of how far we have come, or how far we think we can keep going, determine how we feel about quitting. This might work in the short-term as it is a relief to stop the pain of climbing, but in the long-term, we will only regret the steps we did not take when we still had the opportunity. The only time we should be looking up at what floor level we are standing on is after we have given our absolute best, not when we are looking to measure our progress.

There is a scene from the movie *Facing the Giants* that I believe paints a perfect analogy of this mindset. In the memorable scene, a football coach asks a player to "death crawl" down a field with another player on his back. The player reluctantly agrees and asks the coach, "You want me to go to the 30?" The coach replies that he thinks he can go to the 50-yard line, and even if he can't, he wants the player to give his absolute best. The player, visibly distraught, realizes that he must now go 20 more yards than he originally planned. As the player prepares to crawl, the coach reiterates many times that he wants the player to only give his absolute best.[20]

As the scene continues, the player half-heartedly agrees. Right before the player gets down to crawl, the coach places a blindfold on him. The player asks why, to which the coach responds, "I don't want you giving up at a certain point when you could go further."

As the player begins to crawl down the field, he constantly asks if he has reached the 50-yard line yet. The coach continues to yell in his ear to keep going with only his very best effort. As he continues to push through the pain and moves down the field, the team starts to stand in amazement as he not only passes the 30- and 50-yard line but is almost completely down the field. The player keeps pushing, even though he wants to give up, putting in every ounce of energy he has. When his body finally does give out the coach takes off the blindfold to tell him he has made it to the end zone.[21]

How often are we setting our goals at the 30- or 50-yard line within our "practices" because going any further might not "feel good"? How often are we shorting ourselves of that end zone accomplishment because we want to fall back to what is comfortable? It is easy to look at the end zone or top of the staircase and think it is too much work, but the reality is we can accomplish so much more than we often think, which is exactly why we feel robbed of satisfaction. How much more satisfaction in his achievement did that player have from reaching the end zone in comparison to the 30-yard line he originally wanted to reach? Sure, the work was hard, but the level of satisfaction he gained from seeing what he was capable of far outweighed any temporary satisfaction he would have gained from cheating himself to the 30-yard line.

If we want to train ourselves towards this way of thinking, we must first learn to put on our figurative blind folds and see our work, not as a distant destination, but rather as a series of smaller stair step goals that we can put our very best effort towards. This will help us stop looking at how far we think we can go, or how far we have come, and instead be laser focused on the next step. No longer will our goals be significantly daunting tasks, but rather a series of small steps that we can take until we have reached the top.

A good real-world example of this is looking at a sales representative's goals. When a sales representative is given a quota to reach, it is just like being asked to climb the Burj Khalifa. Reaching the top can be daunting from the bottom. There is no arguing that the goal will be challenging, but how that rep measures himself during the climb makes all the difference. At any moment, the sales representative could find himself looking back at how far he has come and feel "good enough" with his accomplishment, or just as equally look up at how far he still has to go and feel discouraged at the work ahead of him. Either way, the measurement of how far he must go or how far he has come can cause him to step off his "staircase" out of comparison, not out of ability.

This might give the sales rep a sense of satisfaction in the moment, but in both scenarios, his maximized satisfaction was lost because he did not push himself. If, however, he put his blindfold on and climbed each step one at a time giving his absolute best with each sale, then nothing else would matter. Besides stopping at the 50-yard line because he feels he has done just enough, or giving up at the 30-yard line because anything further would feel like too much work, he can eventually find himself in the endzone where his manager can take off his blindfold showing him that he has maximized his satisfaction.

Treasure Chest Goals

Treasure chest goals are a unique set of goals that require a more open-minded approach to their outcome. While most goals have a traditional invest and be rewarded structure, treasure chest goals cannot always guarantee this narrative. That is because the inputs we invest towards treasure chest goals do not always guarantee the outputs we desire. A prime example is setting a goal to get a big promotion. We can work as hard as we want for that promotion, enduring all the challenges, doing all the right things, and overcoming our passion comfort zones, but at the end of the day, the outcome we are working towards is still not guaranteed.

We should view these goals like a treasure chest hunt on an island, hence the name. The island represents our career with the treasure representing the goal we are striving for. It is important to note there is not just one treasure chest buried on the island when it comes to treasure chest goals, there are many different treasure chests scattered across our career, each one containing its own unique loot. To start reaching these goals we approach them like any other goal drawing out a map and plotting our course. Many people will likely chart a course for the biggest treasure on the island and set this goal believing that there is a 100% chance their treasure will be buried at the "X marks the spot." Having this kind of a plan is not a bad mindset to have, but putting all our happiness on the expectation that this treasure will be buried at this spot can be detrimental to our career satisfaction.

After traveling through dangerous jungles, difficult obstacles, and treacherous paths, we begin to eagerly dig for our treasure after reaching the "X." Just like working hard for that promotion and not receiving it, however, there is a chance we may find an empty pit. This, of course, is the opposite of satisfaction, as we are left devastated and disappointed feeling as though our work was wasted. If we are not careful, this disappointment can consume us causing us to question whether or not leaving our passion comfort zone was even worth it.

To overcome this problem, we must understand that treasure chest goals are about anticipating empty pits and plotting alternative courses. By putting all our eggs in one basket, we run the risk of wrecking our satisfaction when so many different treasure chests are still available to us on our island. This does not mean we cannot take a moment to be disappointed in our empty pit of treasure, but if we do not have another X charted on our map in anticipation of this potential outcome, then we will only be left helpless and dissatisfied. By having more than one treasure plotted on our map, we can quickly pick ourselves back up and search for our next possible treasure. An empty pit does not mean our treasure is lost; it just means it is somewhere else to be found.

Anyone who has experienced this type of disappointment knows that encountering an empty pit is inevitable within a career. When it happens, it can be tempting to dig deeper and deeper into our pit hoping the treasure is still there. While it is a good trait to not give up on something we have worked so hard towards, we must utilize this goal to understand when it is time to start looking for the next opportunity of satisfaction. Treasure chest goals are about working hard toward a huge opportunity of satisfaction but also understanding the variability of that outcome. When we embark on our treasure chest hunt knowing our pits have the possibility of being empty, we give ourselves the strength and enthusiasm to set forth on new adventures. In this way, we do not allow ourselves to have a scapegoat back to our comfort zone but rather a plan to work harder towards our "games."

Re-imagined Goals

Holding ourselves accountable to our goals can be daunting, which is why so many people opt not to. While people like the idea of reaching their "games," they often fail to push past the unfavorable circumstances required to reach those opportunities of peak satisfaction. Therefore, it is crucial that we begin applying these re-imagined goals into the "practices" of our career. These goals can help us overcome our temptations to fall back into our passion comfort zones by establishing the need to come pre-prepared to our challenges, keep our eyes only on the step in front of us, and be aware of changing outcomes. Only then will we have the ability to start overcoming our unfavorable circumstances and begin creating consistent satisfaction in our work.

Rule Four:
Expectation Hierarchy

"Expectations were like fine pottery. The harder you held them, the more likely they were to crack."

- Brandon Sanderson

After we have established goals within our career, it is important that we clearly separate those goals from our expectations. While both goals and expectations might seem similar on the surface, the way we believe their outcomes will happen are vastly different. With goals, we understand the outcome we are looking for will require a plan of action and significant effort. With expectations, however, we believe an outcome will occur simply because we want it to, no matter the efforts we put towards it. This makes our belief in our expectations similar to gambling where we are betting on a horse to win a race. By looking at the odds of the horses, we pick an outcome that we believe will happen.

These odds give us the false mentality that we have the power to "plan" our wants. In reality, the outcome of that race is up to pure chance and out of our control. The problem with gambling in our careers is betting these high levels of satisfaction on the role of dice. Therefore, when any expectation goes unmet, we risk derailing ourselves back towards our passion comfort zones. That is why we must learn to balance our expectations alongside our unfavorable circumstances if we are to create a consistently satisfying career.

Surprisingly, this belief that our expectations will happen simply because we want them to is instinctual and something we start doing from a very early age. Jean Piaget, a developmental psychologist, found that children often hold a belief that their thoughts or expectations can cause real results in the world around them.[22] While Piaget suggests that we mostly outgrow this "magical thinking" around the age of seven, it is clear that we carry some matured version of this magical thinking into adulthood. Besides expecting our basketball shoes to magically make us play like Michael Jordan, we instead expect our passions to make our jobs consistently satisfying. This way of thinking can quickly become problematic if not effectively managed within our "practices."

In the article, "The Psychology of Expectations," Dr. John Johnson wrote, "The problem of expectation occurs when we expect something to happen without good reasons for that expectation. If I believe that my expectations alone will bring me what I want, I am using magical thinking and setting myself up for disappointment." [23] Dr. Johnson would go on to further state that "good reason" is the foundation of a healthy expectation.[24] I am not here to imply that we should be writing off "magical thinking" all together, because dreaming is still good for the soul. We should, however, be cautious of how much satisfaction we are investing in these types of "magical" expectations. By utilizing rule four and becoming more aware of the levels of "reason" and "magic" we associate with our expectations, we can mitigate the risks associated with this gambled investment while simultaneously maximizing our odds of satisfaction.

Required, Preferred, and Desired Expectations

Many are familiar with Maslow's Hierarchy of Needs, the theory that people are motivated to fulfill their most basic needs in life, such as finding food, before they can progress towards their more advanced needs like status. I believe our expectations can and should follow a similar path. When looking at traditional expectations, people tend to have an "all or nothing" approach, constantly stacking multiple expectations upon one another for one hopeful outcome. This way of thinking is similar to going all in on a game of poker without the best hand. We understand there is a risk involved but believe in the outcome of winning so much that we are willing to gamble everything we have, even without a royal flush.

While we could certainly still win big from being lucky, we could also lose everything if that expectation goes unmet. Besides taking such a blind "all in" gamble towards our satisfaction, we should instead use a hierarchy of expectations where we can limit our odds of experiencing dissatisfaction.

To do this, we will need to use three levels of expectations: required, preferred, and desired expectations. The first level is to ensure our most basic and important expectations are fulfilled before adding any additional wants to our career. These *required expectations* should be the most grounded in the likelihood of happening and should also follow a "good reason" approach. Next are our *preferred expectations*, the expectations we are willing to compromise on if needed but are still determined to see through. These fall somewhere in the middle of "good reason" and "magical thinking."

Lastly are our *desired expectations*, the expectations we dream about coming true no matter how far-fetched they might seem. These types of expectations fall exclusively under "magical thinking" as the outcomes are often a complete gamble on chance. By using these three levels, we can slowly progress our satisfaction without putting too much weight on one combined outcome. To best explain how these three levels should be used and their impact on our thinking, I will share a hypothetical analogy of a recent college graduate's experience with expectations.

A student was beyond excited when she reached her goal of getting a teaching degree upon graduation. This goal was measurable and achievable through action. It was now time to get a job with that degree. This is where her expectations came into play. She had three specific expectations when it came to finding her first job. She expected her first job to be teaching the 8th grade, that this grade position would be at her number one picked school, and that her first class would be well-behaved.

A traditional mindset would have combined these three expectations into an "all or nothing" approach. The problem with this traditional mindset is that these expectations are not created equally. Some are set in "good reason" while others are set in "magical thinking." Combining all three of these expectations would ultimately cancel out any good reason and put the overall outcome into "magical thinking." This drastically and negatively impacts the odds of her expectations ever happening and would then increase her risk of dissatisfaction.

To best ensure her satisfaction is maximized for her first job, she decided to use the hierarchy of expectations. The hierarchy of expectations dispersed her expectations in a level-up approach where she could prioritize her expected outcomes to have the best odds of satisfaction.

To establish this mindset, she broke down her expectations into the three levels starting with her required expectation. Her required expectation was to become an 8th grade teacher. She knew if she did not end up teaching at an 8th grade level, she would be constantly disappointed, always thinking about the job she wanted most. Therefore, she made sure this expectation was a requirement when looking for jobs.

Next, she established that teaching at the school she wanted most would become a preferred expectation. While this expectation was still especially important to her, she understood her required expectation to teach the 8th grade took precedence over the school where she taught. When she found out that an 8th grade job was not available at the school she wanted most, she did not lose heart as she understood that she now needed to focus on her required expectation. This does not mean the unmet expectation was easy to let go, but without such a compromise prepared, she would have lost two expectations rather than one. In this way, she did not become dissatisfied and lost by combining her expectations but acknowledged where she now needed to invest her energy to ensure her satisfaction.

After landing that first teaching job she had an expectation that her class would be well-behaved. To ensure her satisfaction was maximized, she did not heavily invest her happiness in this outcome becoming true. She understood this expectation was out of her hands and was a complete roll of the dice. Still hopeful, she put forth plans to help influence an outcome of good behavior. While her hopes were high, she did not let the vision of what she wanted determine her happiness. In this way, she could still find satisfaction with a good class while not being overly disappointed with a poorly behaved class.

Required Expectations

Just as the teacher used required expectations to separate what was most important in her career, we too should separate our most important expectations. This allows us to prioritize what we want fulfilled first before considering additional hopes and dreams for our career. A key point to remember is that these expectations, while they can share similarities with treasure chest goals, are still not goals. A treasure chest goal would imply that the outcome can be greatly molded by our actions. While expectations can still be influenced, they are more of a wish rather than a plan. With an expectation, we believe the outcome we want will happen no matter what inputs we do or do not apply. This does not mean we cannot still be persistent towards that outcome though.

Take, for example, the teacher wanting to have an 8th grade class. It does not matter how many credentials and certificates she has or how much planning she puts forth if an 8th grade job is not available. Similarly, even when a job opening is available, she could get passed up by another teacher who has more experience, where again, no amount of action on her part besides time can change that qualification. While she can attempt to influence these outcomes, chance still plays a significant role in this expectation happening. Due to this expectation being a requirement to her satisfaction, however, she will not rest until this expectation is met. While she might not have control over many of the variables, she does have control over her persistence. This persistence will ensure the odds of her expectation significantly increasing, allowing her to progress towards the next two levels of expectations.

Preferred Expectations

Preferred expectations are still crucial to our satisfaction, but the weight we put on them is quite different than required expectations. Preferred expectations are those we are willing to compromise on if the situation calls for it. We still want these outcomes to happen, but we understand their value will always take second place to our required expectations. This means if our preferred expectations are ever connected to our required expectations in a way that will negatively impact them, then we are prepared to compromise. With the new teacher example, she wanted to teach at her number one picked school. It was important to her. Unfortunately, when that preferred school did not have an opening in the grade she wanted, she knew what sacrifice needed to be made.

While this will still cause us some level of disappointment, the alternative option is much worse. Without the hierarchy mindset, the teacher might have decided to take a different grade level job at her preferred school and lost what was most important to her satisfaction, gradually becoming dissatisfied by her inability to prioritize her expectations. With the hierarchy in place, however, she was able to let go of her combined expectations to separate what mattered most. If she had not removed that expectation, then the chain reaction would have caused a line of disappointments leading to her overall dissatisfaction.

Desired Expectations

Our desires are more dreams than anything else because we often project our imaginations onto them. This will cause us to use "magical thinking," which may blind us to any realistic roadblocks we might encounter. Do not be mistaken; "magical thinking" can still be beneficial in inspiring us to dream big and take chances, but the problem with our satisfaction lies in how much weight we put on these expectations coming true. To ensure that we do not fall victim to a series of disappointments from these far-fetched expectations, we must be aware of how much satisfaction we are investing into them.

To do this, we need to train our mind to expect but not count on these outcomes. A great example is gambling on a number in the game of roulette. When placing a bet on a number, we expect that outcome to happen or we would not have placed the bet in the first place. We also recognize that the probability of the ball landing on that number is less than 3%. We are, therefore, smart enough not to bet big by going all in on this expectation. In other words, we expect to win… but we also acknowledge the unlikelihood of that win happening. In this way, we place a bet that allows us to not be devastated from the ball not landing on our number but knowing we can still win big if it does. Investing our satisfaction in desired expectations should be viewed in the same way: betting on it happening, but not investing all our satisfaction on the outcome.

Improving Our Odds

By using these three mindsets of expectations we can better appreciate the constant gambles we make on our satisfaction. If we want to create consistent satisfaction within our careers, then we must be aware of the expectations that we are placing on our challenges and unfavorable circumstances. If we are not properly distributing our "good reason" and "magical thinking" throughout our hierarchy of expectations, then we can fall victim to dissatisfaction outside of our passion comfort zones, tempting us to fall back towards what temporarily "feels good." By using rule four, we give ourselves the opportunity to combat this risk and create the best odds for maximizing our satisfaction.

Rule Five:
Pride In Progress

"There is no happiness except in the realization that we have accomplished something."

- Henry Ford

To this point, we have learned how the previous four rules can help us identify and overcome the unfavorable circumstances of our career. However, simply understanding how to endure our "practices" does not mean those circumstances will suddenly become more enjoyable. If we want to create a consistently satisfying career, then we must learn how to not only overcome our circumstances but find satisfaction through them. How exactly are we supposed to enjoy the unenjoyable? The short answer: We take pride in the progress of our achievements.

Pride, by definition, is a deep pleasure or satisfaction derived from one's own achievements. What better way to find consistent satisfaction throughout our careers than using a tool that allows us to create it through achievement? Our passions, as we learned through rule one, only offer us circumstantial satisfaction, especially if we fail to break free from our passion comfort zones. While our passions can ensure our enjoyment of playing in "games," it still leaves us shorthanded for finding satisfaction in the journey to get there. By utilizing the power of pride, however, we are no longer left hoping that our circumstances play out in our favor but can instead take control of our satisfaction through our own personal achievements.

What I Did vs. Who I Am

Before we can begin the process of discussing pride and its amazing capabilities, we must first address the elephant in the room. Pride, unfortunately, has a shaky reputation and is not always viewed in a positive light. The power of pride has been misused by the wrong people; misused because it is a person's decision on whether its power is directed towards good or evil. That is because the power of pride and its influence on satisfaction is 100% dependent on the type of pride a person uses. On one hand, a person can use pride to create immense amounts of satisfaction in his/her work through productivity and motivation of achievement. On the other hand, pride can be used for arrogance and selfishness causing destruction rather than creation. If we want to ensure our long-term satisfaction, then we must first examine these two extremes, so we do not misuse them within our career.

How do we ensure that we use the right type of pride? It starts by drawing a clear line between the two. Fortunately, psychologists Jessica Tracey and Richard Robins have clearly separated these two "facets," as they call them, so we may better understand their structure. As Tracey and Robins state, pride can either be "authentic" or "hubristic." Authentic pride most closely resembles our idea of "good pride" where we find satisfaction in the expression of our work.[25] For example, "I won because I practiced," therefore, "I'm proud of what I did." [26] Hubristic pride resembles our idea of "bad pride" or self-centered pride.[27] This pride is less about the satisfaction in something we worked toward and more about the inflated vision of who we think we are.[28] For example, "I won because I'm always great," therefore, "I'm proud of what I am".[29]

Understanding the differences between authentic and hubristic pride can help guide us towards the correct use of pride's abilities. If at any moment we find ourselves thinking we are proud of who we are, not of what we did, then we must make an immediate change in our use of pride. While hubristic pride can still create a sense of momentary satisfaction, it will eventually cause more harm than good. When we lean towards hubristic pride, we believe that we are better than our circumstances, once again causing us to risk walking away from our passions. With authentic pride, we seek to conquer our circumstances to create satisfaction from our achievements not our interests. Pride in progress is not about being proud in the type of work we do; it is about being proud in the type of obstacles we can overcome. It is only after we have made this distinction between the two facets of pride that we can begin finalizing our path to a consistently satisfying career.

Pride In Progress

Now that we are aware of authentic pride, we must understand how to properly use it. Authentic pride is not about waiting to experience satisfaction at the end of our work (ie: games), rather it is about finding satisfaction in the progress we have made to get there. If we just waited until we won our "games" to be satisfied, we would miss so many opportunities of satisfaction along the way. Consistent career satisfaction is just as much about finding pride during our practices as it is in winning our games.

There is a commonly known, but unattributed, story about three masons that I believe paints a perfect picture of what pride in progress really looks like. The story goes as such:

A man comes across three masons chipping away large blocks of granite in a quarry. The man walking by became intrigued as to why these three masons were doing this, so he decided to ask each mason why they were chipping away at the granite.

As the man walked up to the first mason, he could tell he was unhappy. He had a constant frown on his face, always looking at his watch. When he asked this mason what he was doing, the mason responded by saying, "I am hammering these stupid blocks; I just can't wait till it's 5 o'clock so I can go home."

Without a real answer to his question, the man walked towards the second mason hoping for a better explanation. This mason seemed to have more energy in his step, yet still lacked interest and enthusiasm in his work. Approaching the second mason, the man asked the same question about what he was doing to which the second mason responded, "I am breaking these blocks of granite apart so they may be used for building blocks. It's not bad work, but I'll sure be glad when it's done."

Still with no answer to his curiosity, the man walked to the third mason. This mason was chipping away at the granite in a very productive and precise manner. He seemed to be far more energized and motivated than the other two. As the man got closer, he realized this mason would occasionally stop, stand back, and admire his progress with a big grin on his face. As the man reached this mason to ask what he was doing, the third mason responded with the simple statement, "I'm building a beautiful cathedral!"

What is great about this story is that it shows us the many different impacts our mindsets of pride can have on our work. It shows that our work ethic, attitude, and overall satisfaction can be dramatically impacted by our perception of the task at hand. That is why there are three different feelings of satisfaction all coming from the same exact job. Each mason is doing an unfavorable task, but each mason has made a choice on how to view his work, which created significant ripple effects in not only his satisfaction in the task, but his drive to complete it.

This shows that we can either pout about the work we don't consider to be our passion, break through our passion comfort zone but still only focus on our "games," or break through our passion comfort zone while simultaneously creating satisfaction in the progress of our work. By picking apart this story, we can better educate ourselves on how and why pride in progress is so crucial for creating a consistently satisfying career.

Three Mindsets

While all three masons were not doing work they were passionate about, the third mason was able to find satisfaction in his work. To understand why, we must look at how the first and second mason are perceiving their unfavorable task. The first mason clearly had no interest in his work and was only focused on how the task at hand felt like a chore. He did not see his work as practice or an investment towards a bigger goal. All this mason was concerned about was the fact that in that exact moment he was not doing what he was passionate about. He was outside of his passion comfort zone and not seeing any reward in doing something he was not interested in, only to be left unsatisfied by his own demise (relying on passion alone).

The second mason was trying to break through his passion comfort zone by viewing his work as practice and the completion of his work as his game. He understood his task at hand might not be his passion but could still see the potential reward of reaching the end goal. This, however, caused him to focus only on the future or his "game" and not create satisfaction throughout the process. By saying, "I'll sure be glad when it's done," he limits his satisfaction to only the end goal. While this mason still finds more satisfaction in his work than the first mason, he still comes up short in comparison to the third mason because he is failing to find consistent satisfaction along the way. All he sees is a destination to his work (only finding satisfaction in "games").

The third mason was not thinking of his work as a chore outside of his passion or a means of simply reaching his "game." Instead, this mason saw his work as an opportunity to find pride and, therefore, satisfaction in the progress of his work. It did not matter if he was or was not passionate about breaking blocks because the self-satisfaction he received from beautifully crafting each piece was a reward in and of itself. Like a painter stepping back to admire the progress of his painting, the mason stepped back to constantly admire how each completed block slowly formed the bigger picture of his achievement.

He had overcome the temptation to break free from his passion comfort zone, saw the "game" he was investing in, set gradual goals that helped him progress his pride, and anticipated any unrealistic expectations he might have along the way. Unlike the other two masons, his satisfaction was not based on simply doing what he was passionate about, nor was it based on waiting to play in his "game." This mason's satisfaction was based on the pride he gained from a constant job well done (taking pride in the progress of his "practice").

Power Over Circumstances

It is one thing to read an analogy about the impact pride in progress can have on our way of thinking, it is another to understand the science behind it. How realistic is it that someone like the third mason could truly find consistent satisfaction and motivation by simply taking pride in overcoming their unfavorable circumstances? A study, completed by psychologists Lisa Williams and David DeSteno at Northeastern University, can help us understand just how realistic this scenario is. Williams and DeSteno conducted two separate studies that looked at the impact pride had on motivational behaviors (passion comfort zones) during specific unfavorable tasks (non-passions). In doing so, they measured the level of perseverance and persistence participants had in unfavorable tasks based on what type of mindset they used.[30] The results they found can show us just how much power pride gives us over our circumstances.

Pride Alters Behavior

The first study looked at the impact pride has on our behaviors of motivation. It is easy to think of pride as a simple cause and effect, but this study showed that there is more happening from our actions than just a belated output of satisfaction. Within their study, Williams and DeSteno monitored the differing levels of motivation and perseverance that took place when constant pride was taken in one's work. What they found was that those who took pride in the progress of their unfavorable tasks were able to create a new sense of motivation and perseverance outside of their typical boundaries of passion.[31] The participants who took pride in their work outperformed and outworked those who did not take pride in their work even though all participants were not interested in the task at hand.[32]

In other words, those who took pride in the progress of their work had more drive to take on the tasks at hand even though it was not their interest, showing us that pride helped them power through the boundaries of their passion comfort zones. Williams and DeSteno stated that the results "provide some of the first evidence supporting a functional influence of pride on behavior." [33] They continued by saying, "pride appears to have motivated individuals to exert greater effort on a taxing task."[34] This, of course, is a big deal when it comes to understanding the power of pride over our circumstances. This study shows us that we no longer have to be mentally held back by our unfavorable circumstances but can take control of our perseverance and motivation through the use of pride as we seek the satisfaction that follows our achievements.

Pride > Positive Attitude

Following this study, Williams and DeSteno wanted to ensure that positive thinking was not influencing their participants' work and results, but that it was pride alone creating this sense of perseverance. To do this, they studied how positive thinking in contrast to pride influenced participants' behaviors on unfavorable tasks. What is notable about this study is that positive thinking, or having a positive attitude, is a commonly used tool taught to those struggling to find satisfaction or motivation in their work. When people are having a hard time enjoying their unfavorable tasks, it seems the first go-to response is, "just be positive." As it turns out, this is not only a temporary fix to our satisfaction, but seemingly ineffective towards our overall work ethic.

While positive thinking is still an important aspect to finding career satisfaction, this study found that it cannot and does not change our natural drive of reward in the same way pride does.[35] As the study found, there was a significantly greater impact in participants' perseverance with the use of pride in contrast to those with just a positive attitude.[36] The psychologists found that "positive mood was not a viable mechanism for producing increased perseverance" adding that "positive mood did not produce greater perseverance on a taxing task, pride did."[37] This shows us that the old methods of preaching "positive thinking" towards unfavorable tasks might not hold as much weight as we once thought to improving our career satisfaction.

While having a positive attitude is still a must, relying on it alone, just like passion, will not offer us the power we need over our circumstances. In fact, as this study suggests, positive thinking does not even improve our motivation, it is pride alone that drives us past our most unfavorable challenges. This shows us that pride not only motivates us further than positive thinking, but creates a sense of satisfaction more desirable than positive thinking. In doing so, our perseverance to reach that level of satisfaction pushes us through some of our most unfavorable tasks. Without pride we have no determination to reach our achievements, without those achievements we have no satisfaction over our unfavorable tasks, without that satisfaction we will inevitably fail to achieve a consistently satisfying career.

Pride Over Passion

Pride - prīd

noun

A feeling or deep pleasure or satisfaction *derived from one's own achievements*

While following our passion will still be a necessary step towards enjoying our career, we must remember that its effects of satisfaction will always be variable to our circumstances. Our passions might help us find what "game" we want to play in but, as we have learned, this opportunity of peak satisfaction will only account for a fraction of our career. Even the most picture-perfect careers will come with their fair share of unsatisfying and unfavorable circumstances. If we do not want our satisfaction to be held back from these circumstances, then it is imperative that we start utilizing rule five within our career.

Rule five builds off the previous four rules of overcoming our unfavorable circumstances and allows us to create a unique sense of satisfaction from those achievements. When we start to take pride in the progress of our work, we start to alter our overall work experience. Our pride motivates us to invest in challenges, pushes us towards a new level of perseverance, and rewards us with satisfaction in the process. This behavioral mind shift causes us to desire work that we can be proud of conquering, work that might not always be our direct interest but work that is worth overcoming to achieve satisfaction. Therefore, our careers become less about expecting to "never working a day in your life" and more about "working to enjoy every day of your life." If we are capable of this skill, then we will see the amazing power of prioritizing pride over passion.

Closing Remarks

"Practice makes perfect, and you will learn and find solutions in ways you never imagined possible."

— Jo Bradford

You cannot expect to read this book once, set it on a shelf to collect dust, and walk away believing that you now have the ability to create a consistently satisfying career. The knowledge of this book is only as good as the actions you take upon reading it. *That is because knowledge without application is worthless and application without practice is pointless.* To get the most out of this book will require putting together tangible plans on how you want to apply and practice each of the five rules. Maybe that means putting sticky notes on each rule to reference them when you need them most, maybe it means focusing on individual rules each day of the week, or maybe it means writing down your daily unfavorable circumstances in a journal to plan out how to overcome them when they are re-encountered. Whatever it is that you choose to do, your ability to create consistent satisfaction lies in your discipline of applying and practicing these rules daily within your career.

Has this book made a difference in your career?

I would love to hear from you! Send me an email at: **PrideOverPassion@gmail.com** and tell me your story of overcoming career dissatisfaction using these five rules.

Acknowledgments

I want to start off by thanking God for my undeserved blessings that have allowed me to write this book. Only by His grace and blessed opportunities does this book exist today.

Speaking of blessings, I must thank my incredible wife, Karin Ingle. Karin, your tremendous support of my goals and aspirations has allowed me the opportunity to write and publish this book. You are my rock and my cheerleader; without your support I would not have been able to reach many of my goals and accomplishments in life. Karin, you are my one true love, and I am so thankful for all that you do. I am grateful to call you my wife and life partner; I love you more than you will ever know.

I would like to thank my Dad, John Ingle, who was also the mentor I mentioned in the introduction that inspired me to not only work on improving my career satisfaction but also work hard in life. Dad, you have always been the key person I look up to in life and in work. The professionalism and hard work ethic you set as an example has always driven me to do the same. I am grateful that I was able to gain your support and input on this book. I could not ask for a better father and role model in my life.

Nancy Carlson, my mother-in-law, was also a huge help in the completion of this book. Nancy, thank you for taking time out of your day to not only help me complete the first-round of edits but also add helpful insights so that my writing style could be improved. If it was not for some of your ideas and recommendations this book would not have come together the way it did. Thank you for your support in helping make this book become a reality.

Next, I want to thank Josie Luedke, my high school English teacher. Josie, I am honored that you selflessly took time out your busy schedule of teaching and being a full-time mom to help me complete this book. I am fortunate to have had such an influential teacher who helped teach me many of the skills I needed to write this book, as well as become an inspiration for my love of writing. Thank you for all your help, it was greatly appreciated.

I want to thank Elise Gallagher, the final editor of this book. Elise, thank you for your professionalism and attention to detail. It is because of your efforts that I was able to confidently publish this book knowing I had a great editor to partner with. I am grateful to have worked alongside you with this project. (*If you are looking to have any professional editing work done, I highly recommend reaching out to Elise through her Reedsy profile: reedsy.com/elise-gallagher*)

I want to also thank Chris Schatzman for his incredible design skills on this book cover. Your ability to create eye catching and memorable art is something I envy. Thank you for your hard work, creativity, and being a pleasure to work with. (*If you are looking to have any type of graphic design work done at any scale, I highly recommend reaching out to Chris at: studioequinox@earthlink.net*)

Lastly, I want to thank you, the reader. There are millions of books out there, but you chose to purchase and read this one. These five rules towards improving career satisfaction are something I have always been eager to share on a large scale since their conception, so I am grateful to have had this opportunity to share them with you. I hope they make as big of an impact in your career as they have in mine and allow you to find a rewarding and consistently satisfying career.

Thank you,
Drew Ingle

NOTES

Introduction

1   Clifton, J. (2017, June 13) The World's Broken Workplace. *Gallup*. Retrieved from https://news.gallup.com/opinion/chairman/212045/worldbrokenworkplace.aspx?g_source=&g_medium=related&g_campaign=tiles

2   Kan, M., Levanon, G., Li, A., & Ray, R. L. (2017). *Job Satisfaction* (2017 ed., p. 5, Publication). New York, NY: The Conference Board.

3   Hellebuyck, M., Nguyen, T., Halphern, M., Fritze, D., & Kennedy, J. (2017). *Mind The Workplace* (pp. 18-19, Publication). Alexandria, VA: Mental Health America.

Rule One: Don't Rely On Passion Alone

4-9   O'Keefe, P. A., Dweck, C. S., & Walton, G. M. (2018). Implicit Theories of Interest: Finding Your Passion or Developing It? *Psychological Science, 29*(10), 16531664. doi:10.1177/0956797618780643

10-12   Theories of Motivation. (n.d.). Retrieved November 2, 2019, from https://courses.lumenlearning.com/boundless-psychology/chapter/theories-of-motivation/

Rule Two: 95% Practice 5% Game

13-16 Forstall, S., Fadell, T., & Christie, G. (2017, June 29). Apple's Secret iPhone Launch Team: The Event That Began It All [Interview]. Retrieved 2019, from https://www.youtube.com/watch?v=xxBc1c3uAJw&feature=youtu.be

Rule Three: Set Goals

17 The Harvard MBA Business School Study on Goal Setting. (2016, April 18). Retrieved 2020, from https://www.wanderlustworker.com/the-harvard-mba-business school-study-on-goal-setting/

18 Brunstein, J. C., Schultheiss, O. C., & Grässman, R.(1998). Personal goals and emotional well-being: The moderating role of motive dispositions. Journal of Personality and Social Psychology, 75(2), 494–508. https://doi.org/10.1037/00223514.75.2.494

19 The Harvard MBA Business School Study on Goal Setting. (2016, April 18). Retrieved 2020, from https://www.wanderlustworker.com/the-harvard-mba-business school-study-on-goal-setting/

20-21 Kendrick, S., Kendrick, A., & Nixon, D. (Producers), & Kendrick, A. (Director). (2006).*Facing the Giants* [Motion picture]. United States: Sherwood Pictures, Provident Films, Caramel Entertainment, Kendrick Brothers Group

Rule Four: Expectation Hierarchy

22-24 Johnson, J. A. (2018, February 17). The Psychology of Expectations. Retrieved from https://www.psychology today.com/us/blog/cui-bono/201802/the-psychology expectations

Rule Five: Pride In Progress

25-29 Tracy, J. L., & Robins, R. W. (2007). The Psychological Structure of Pride: A Tale of Two Facets. [Abstract]. *Journal of Personality and Social Psychology, 92*(3), 507. doi:10.1037/0022-3514.92.3.506

30-37 Williams, L. A., & Desteno, D. (2008). Pride and Perseverance: The Motivational Role of Pride. *Journal of Personality and Social Psychology, 94*(6), 1007-1017. doi:10.1037/0022-3514.94.6.1007

Did You Enjoy This Book?

Please leave a review on Amazon and share with friends and colleagues!

Emails sent to PrideOverPassion@gmail.com may not all receive a response but will be personally reviewed and looked over by Drew Ingle

2 Corinthians 5:7

Copyright © 2021 by Drew Ingle. All rights reserved.

Made in the USA
Monee, IL
24 February 2021